To Barbara

Joseph Buloff as Ivan in the Harold Clurman Theatre production of The Chekhov Sketchbook

THE CHEKHOV SKETCHBOOK

THE VAGABOND

THE WITCH

IN A MUSIC SHOP

Three short stories by
Anton Chekhov
dramatized by

Luba Kadison and Joseph Buloff

No part of this book may be reproduced, stored in a retrieval system, or transmitted in any form, by any means, including mechanical, electronic, photocopying, recording, or otherwise, without the prior written permission of the publisher.

SAMUEL FRENCH, INC.
45 WEST 25TH STREET   NEW YORK 10010
7623 SUNSET BOULEVARD   HOLLYWOOD 90046
LONDON   *TORONTO*

Copyright ©, 1980, 1982, by Luba Kadison and Joseph Buloff

ALL RIGHTS RESERVED

CAUTION: Professionals and amateurs are hereby warned that THE CHEKHOV SKETCHBOOK is subject to a royalty. It is fully protected under the copyright laws of the United States of America, the British Commonwealth, including Canada, and all other countries of the Copyright Union. All rights, including professional, amateur, motion pictures, recitation, lecturing, public reading, radio broadcasting, television, and the rights of translation into foreign languages are strictly reserved. In its present form the play is dedicated to the reading public only.

ALL of the plays contained in THE CHEKHOV SKETCHBOOK may be given stage presentation by amateurs (on the same bill) upon a collective royalty of Fifty Dollars for the first performance, and Thirty-Five Dollars for each additional performance. If performed separately by amateurs the royalty is Twenty Dollars for the first performance, and Fifteen Dollars for each additional performance, **per play**. *Fees are payable one week before the date of production to Samuel French, Inc., at 45 West 25th Street, New York, N.Y. 10010, or at 7623 Sunset Boulevard, Hollywood, Calif. 90046, or to Samuel French (Canada), Ltd., 80 Richmond Street East, Toronto, Ontario, Canada M5C 1P1.*

Royalty of the required amount must be paid whether the play is presented for charity or gain and whether or not admission is charged.

Stock royalty quoted on application to Samuel French, Inc.

For all other rights than those stipulated above, apply to Samuel French, Inc.

Particular emphasis is laid on the question of amateur or professional readings, permission and terms for which must be secured in writing from Samuel French, Inc.

Copying from this book in whole or in part is strictly forbidden by law, and the right of performance is not transferable.

Whenever the play is produced the following notice must appear on all programs, printing and advertising for the play: "Produced by special arrangement with Samuel French, Inc."

Due authorship credit must be given on all programs, printing and advertising for the play.

Anyone presenting the play shall not commit or authorize any act or omission by which the copyright of the play or the right to copyright same may be impaired.

No changes shall be made in the play for the purpose of your production unless authorized in writing.

The publication of this play does not imply that it is necessarily available for performance by amateurs or professionals. Amateurs and professionals considering a production are strongly advised in their own interests to apply to Samuel French, Inc., for consent before starting rehearsals, advertising, or booking a theatre or hall.

Printed in U.S.A.

ISBN 0 573 60045 7

THE CHEKHOV SKETCHBOOK was produced by the Harold Clurman Theater at 412 West 42nd St., N.Y.C., Jack Garfein, Artistic Director. It started previews on Sat., Oct. 25, opened on Nov. 9, 1980 and closed on Jan. 25, 1981, for a total of 106 performances.

Jack Garfein
Artistic Director

presents

THE CHEKHOV SKETCHBOOK

translated and adapted by
Luba Kadison and Joseph Buloff

starring
(in alphabetical order)

| PENELOPE ALLEN | JOSEPH BULOFF | JOHN HEARD | STEPHEN D. NEWMAN |

with

Frank Bara   Jack O'Connell

| *Setting by* | *Costumes by* | *Lighting by* | *Sound by* |
| Hugh Landwehr | David Murin | Frances Aronson | George Hansen |

Stage Manager
Johnna Murray

Directed by
Tony Giordano

In addition, Mr. Joseph Buloff has toured with these plays to Chicago, Buenos Aires, Rio de Janeiro, and numerous cities in France and Israel.

All three plays are set in Russia, c. 1870.

I

THE VAGABOND

Characters:

VAGABOND

NIK (Nikander)

PTAKH

I

THE VAGABOND

A gloomy late autumn sky overlooks a sodden road flanked by some scattered and tortured-looking trees. On the Left side a few naked trees lie on top of each other. Center a twin tree of which one part is sawed off to a stump that forms a seat. A similar stump of a cut tree is on the Right side.

A shabby little figure in torn and tattered clothes with chains running from his waist to both his ankles enters Upstage Right. Burying his head in his collar he slowly ambles across the Stage and disappears Stage Left. As he disappears, PTAKH, *square, squat, with a beard, recognizable by his worn uniform as a policeman, follows him on. He seems to be searching for a dry leaf on the ground. When he reaches the Center of the Stage he looks back to where he came from.*

PTAKH. Hey, Nik, did you find any?
NIK. (*From Offstage*) God damn it . . . I got trouble.
PTAKH. What happened?

(NIK, *a second policeman, tall, heavy, enters limping.*)

PTAKH. (*Continued*) What's the matter with you?
NIK. Damn it. Look at that. I tried to jump the puddle . . . and I ripped the sole right off my boot . . . Now it's lapping up the slime like a thirsty horse.

THE VAGABOND

PTAKH. That's great. We only have thirty miles ahead of us . . .

NIK. What muck. It sticks to your boots like tar.

PTAKH. I knew this morning the rain would get us. Here when it rains a day you can't find a dry leaf for a month.

NIK. I have to pour this slush out of my boot.

PTAKH. I knew the rain would get us.

(NIK *sits on the cut trees, tries to take off his boot*)

PTAKH. (*Continued*) Come on, I'll help you . . .

(PTAKH, *his back to* NIK, *takes* NIK'S *foot between his legs.* NIK *pushes* PTAKH *in the rear to free his foot.* PTAKH *suddenly realizes the chained man is far Offstage. He yells*)

Hey, you, come back here! What's your hurry, you scum! Get back here . . . Back I say!

(*He goes on searching on the ground*)

NIK. My wife, may she roast in hell forever, promised to knit me a pair of woolen bindings to wrap my feet . . . that slut! The last few pennies she drinks away . . . the windows are broken . . . the roof is leaking . . . the children run around hungry in the cold . . . tell you the truth, I'm glad to be out of the house for a day or two . . . But to walk on this damn road . . .

PTAKH. (*As the chained man re-enters*) Sit down. Give your chains a rest. You have a long road ahead of you . . . Sit down I say!

(*The man sits down slowly on the stump under the middle tree*)

NIK. I'm dying for a smoke.

PTAKH. (*Taking out a small sack from his pocket*) Can't find a scrap of paper . . . I have plenty of tobacco . . . but there isn't a single dry leaf to roll it in.

NIK. (*Showing the torn boot*) Look at that . . . In this muck the strongest boots would fall apart . . . And there she drinks away my last penny . . . I hate to come home at night . . . There is no kerosene in the lamp . . . she lies dead drunk . . . I even have to warm my own plate in the dark . . . May lightning strike her dead, the slut!

PTAKH. You think mine is better? Carries on with that ugly runt — the carpenter, Petroff . . .

NIK. I thought of telling you that too . . .

PTAKH. I caught her once in bed with that lousy midget . . . I hit him right over the head with the poker. He ran out in his underpants, screaming to the moon for help.

NIK. (*Laughing*) That's good . . .

PTAKH. I would like to give her a taste of the poker too . . . But you know her . . . a wild beast. She grabbed me by the beard . . . I thought she'd tear my face off my head. And what hurts most, I couldn't even moan or groan in pain . . . I had to keep smiling . . . It would make people laugh: some policeman, can't even keep order in his own house. Oh yes, brother . . . Just keep your mouth shut. Choke but don't talk . . . (*Still looking around for a dry leaf on the ground*)

NIK. Say! . . . I just thought of something . . . we have paper . . . the transport orders for that creep.

(*Takes off his cap where he keeps the orders*)

PTAKH. Don't we have to bring it back stamped and signed by the police commissioner?

NIK. We can use a little piece of this. Who'll give a damn? It's only a few words . . . (*Points to paper*)

PTAKH. Not a bad idea. There's plenty of empty space down here. (*Looks dumbly into paper*) They may not even know the difference.

NIK. Rip it from the bottom.

PTAKH. (*Turning the paper upside down*) I wish I knew which *is* the bottom.

NIK. Just leave the writing part. Take it from the side . . . Wipe your hands! Don't mess it up!

PTAKH. (*Tears it*) That'll do . . .

(PTAKH *gives the rest of the paper back to* NIK, *who places it under his hat.* PTAKH *carefully tears the scrap into several parts*)

We'll ration it carefully. We have a long night ahead of us . . . It's good paper and first class tobacco . . . Why didn't we think of it before? (*Sits down on stump Left*) This will be something really good.

(*The* VAGABOND *looks at the two policemen lighting their cigarettes and smoking with great delight*)

VAGABOND. Say, Captain, would you save a puff for me?

PTAKH. (*Turns and looks disgustedly at the chained little man*) Shut up, you bum! Look at that. It talks. A puff he'd like. Perhaps you'd like a real cigar.

(NIK *laughs*)

PTAKH. (*Continued*) I can't understand what makes them bother with those tramps when they could get rid of them with one good bullet in their rear or a little rope around their neck — but no. Drag them to Siberia — what for? Who needs them? Eh you, I'm talking to you.

ACT I   THE VAGABOND   11

(*The* VAGABOND *doesn't answer.*

The policemen laugh. NIK *turns to* PTAKH)

NIK. So what happened to your carpenter?
PTAKH. He wouldn't dare show up when I'm around . . . I'm sure of that! But now that I've been dragging this tramp on the road since early morning, who knows? A woman is a woman always. (*To the* VAGABOND) Hey you! Pipsqueak. Are you married? I am asking you.

(*The* VAGABOND *shakes his head*)

NIK. Tramps have all the luck!
PTAKH. That's right.
NIK. (*To the* VAGABOND) I'm going to catch cold in this Goddamned slush. Or even rheumatism in my leg with an open boot like this!
VAGABOND. You're not blaming me for that. I didn't tear your boots.
NIK. Who else? When we get you to the next town and hand you over to the local police they'll let you rest for a week or so in a nice, cosy jail before they take you further . . . But we—we'll have to drag ourselves back through these darn swamps the very same night.
VAGABOND. I can't help that. That's the law of the land. No homeless tramp without papers was ever sent to Siberia in a carriage with white horses.
NIK. All tramps think they know the law of the land.
VAGABOND. Oh, I know many things.
PTAKH. Yeah, you know everything except your own name.
VAGABOND. (*Proudly*) I even know how to read and write . . .
PTAKH. (*To* NIK) Eh! Listen to that! (*To the* VAGABOND) What else do you know?

VAGABOND. Many, many things.

PTAKH. Many things. Are you trying to tell us you're anything but a lousy tramp?

VAGABOND. I'm not exactly a tramp — nor am I particularly lousy.

PTAKH. Then why didn't you tell them your name when they asked you?

VAGABOND. I don't remember.

(POLICEMEN *laugh lightly*)

NIK. Even a dog remembers his name . . . Since morning I've been trying to guess what the name of such a bag of bones would be.

VAGABOND. What difference would it make to you?

NIK. How about telling *us* your name? You don't have to fear us . . . We are just simple people and don't give a rap what your name may be . . . What is your name? Don't tell us you never had a name.

VAGABOND. I don't have it . . . No name.

PTAKH. So who are you? Where do you come from?

NIK. You're a Christian, aren't you?

VAGABOND. I'm surely not a Tartar or a Turk.

PTAKH. Then you were christened? Hum?

VAGABOND. Of course. I go to church. I take the sacrament. I wouldn't touch a crust of bread on a fast day even if I were starving. I sometimes even go to church to light a candle for the soul of my mother and in need I even pray to Heaven for some help.

PTAKH. Then what's your Christian name? Tell us. Nobody will hear. Come on, come on . . . if you had a mother she no doubt called you by a name.

(VAGABOND *shrugs*)

NIK. Don't tell us you never had a mother either.

ACT I THE VAGABOND 13

PTAKH. That's a good one. (*Laughs heartily*)

VAGABOND. I certainly had a mother.

NIK. Then she must have called you by a name.

VAGABOND. I told you . . . I don't remember.

PTAKH. You mean you'd rather not remember. Who was your mother? A bum? A slut? A public whore?

VAGABOND. Oh, God forbid! She was a decent, honest woman . . .

NIK. And brought up a wretch like you?

PTAKH. No mother? What about your father? Talk — don't be scared — they cannot send you further than Siberia.

VAGABOND. (*After a moment*) My mother was a servant girl in the house of a rich landowner in the south where the Volga flows into the sea. He was a baron of Latvian descent and if you insist on knowing who my father was I can in total and complete sincerity assure you that my father was none other than that Latvian baron. You may not believe it but I was born in a crystal white palace by the shores of the Black Sea. As a child I slept on silk pillows of softest down. In the morning I was fed little white rolls and hot chocolate. I wore velvet knickers, long, silk socks, and shoes with pink suede buttons, as befits a child of noble birth. My father would shower my mother with gifts of large boxes of fruit and candy . . . and believe me, my friends, for the number of chocolates and pastries that I consumed in my childhood I could have bought a good foursome carriage with carved and colored wheels. My mother, blessed be her soul, scrubbed the floors of my father's palace . . . but for me it was candy, chocolate, and books . . . I never knew where she got the books. Perhaps she sneaked them from my father's extraordinary library. My mother would do anything so that I would not grow up an illiterate peasant like herself. Everything that you see in me and what I am I owe to my dear mother and those wonderful books . . . She would not allow me to use obscenity, or even speak the vulgar Russian language. Instead, she made me read and learn how to speak French . . . "Bonjour, monsieur — comment allez-vous? — Parlez-vous francais? Comme ci, comme ça, monsieur." She taught me how to wear beautiful clothes . . . and how to behave in the society to which I belonged by virtue of the noble blood flowing in my veins . . . If she's still alive somewhere may God grant her long, long years . . . But if her soul is gone may the good earth keep her tormented body in sweet repose . . . Had it not been for my saintly mother I would have come into the world a lowly peasant and would have remained a peasant for the rest of my life . . . But thanks to her blessed soul you may ask me any questions you like about people, countries, cities, even about God — I have the answers to all of them . . . She herself carried the garbage slops every day, but she taught me to live with grace — in decency and cleanliness. While other people engage in debauchery and drunken brawls, with hatred in their hearts, I can always pick up a slim volume, sit myself in a small corner and enjoy a good cry . . . You have no idea what touching stories you find in books. Tears run down my cheeks and my heart fills with pity and compassion for all people and even for myself . . . And I feel good. Very good . . . If only you were able to read you'd know what I mean.

PTAKH. Aww, bosh! We've heard all about these books . . . You certainly don't look like a real nobleman — and I know you're not an honest peasant — so what are you?

NIK. Where's your father now?

VAGABOND. My father?

NIK. Yes, the same father you told us about.

VAGABOND. Unfortunately, I hardly knew him . . . All I remember is that he was a rich nobleman of very high

ACT I   THE VAGABOND   15

rank . . . My mother, after all, was just a servant girl . . . and you know, my dear friends, that a servant girl cannot always resist the will of her master.

PTAKH. Ah-hah! That whole fine story makes you nothing but a bastard.

VAGABOND. Well, in a certain sense I would say you could call me that. Perhaps on certain nights my mother did sin, but it was exactly through her sin that I was elevated to my present station. My origin is no longer of the common peasant but of the noblest landed gentry.

NIK. Well, if you are such an aristocrat, why are you afraid to tell your name?

VAGABOND. Why should I? Had you let me go free it would perhaps be different — but in chains, my name can only increase my punishment . . . As it is I'm just a tramp without a home, father, mother, papers, passports, name or certificates; and therefore, according to the law, being sent on foot to Siberia for life.

PTAKH. That's right! Don't tell your name! But in Siberia, you think they'll meet you with an orchestra? The first day they'll tear your pants down and treat you to a hundred lashes.

VAGABOND. No, fifty. That's the law. But had I given my true identity they would have locked me up once more in a black dungeon and then again sent me deep down into the dark coal mines. Oh, I know the law.

NIK. Why do you say again? Have you been in jail before?

VAGABOND. Not once but three times. The last time for eight years. With a shaved head and with chains twice as heavy as these I was tearing huge chunks of coal from the earth and carrying them on my back — for miles.

NIK. Why?

PTAKH. What did you do? Kill someone? A squirt like you?

VAGABOND. I was a little boy when my mother put a deadly drop of poison in my father's wine.

NIK. I'll be damned . . .

PTAKH. I knew all the time his mother was a bitch.

VAGABOND. I beg you please don't besmirch her name. She was a pure and saintly woman . . . But who can tell? . . . The heart of a woman is like a deep dark forest. Who can enter there and not be lost? Perhaps she did it by mistake. And then again perhaps she simply could not bear the pain in her heart when my father took a new servant girl into his bed . . . I was a child. How could I be expected to understand any of it? All I remember is that we were condemned by court. My mother for twenty years and I for seven.

PTAKH. I can understand your mother. But where in the hell do you come in?

VAGABOND. I was always an obedient child and helped my mother. She asked me to serve the glass of wine to my father. How could I have known? I often brought his tea or coffee to his bed . . . Look, fellows, you made me talk. I was talking to you as if I were talking to God himself. I hope you never, never get the thought of betraying me . . .

PTAKH. Why should we? We have plenty of our own trouble.

VAGABOND. One word from you and I'm back in prison.

NIK. What word? Which word? You talked and talked and we still don't even know your name.

VAGABOND. How could I ever disclose my name? I'm asking you as my own brothers. In a minute they would lock me up once more behind iron bars.

PTAKH. Once more? You mean you have escaped? . . .

VAGABOND. That's not entirely true. By nature I'm not a jail breaker . . . I was just following the others. I had to! . . . We were eighteen in a room! How they got the keys or broke the locks I'll never know, but I had to follow them for I am the least and last fit for the hard and cruel labor there. I'm a delicate creature, a sensitive soul. I need a clean, soft bed to sleep, a fresh, clean tablecloth when I'm served a meal. I was born an aristocrat. No man can free himself from what he is. Now, Siberia, I don't mind. I have no fear of Siberia . . . After all, Siberia is part of our country. The same skies . . . the same God . . . only better . . . much . . . much . . . better.

PTAKH. (*Laughing*) You still think they'll take you to a picnic in Siberia?

VAGABOND. In jail you're a mangy dog in hell. To be trapped and jammed in with brutes and cut-throats reeking of filth, spitting on the floor, urinating on the walls. Not even a corner to kneel and raise your eyes to Heaven. Oh no, your honor. Not for me. But Siberia, my dear friends — that's a place for people of my breed: writers, teachers, poets, philosophers, the sharpest minds, the most distinguished names . . . ask me and I will tell you. I studied all of it carefully in my childhood. (*Pause*) You see, when they send you to Siberia for life, they give you a little hut and a piece of land around it. In fact, you can have as much land as you want, because land is cheap as snow there. And don't worry, brothers, I will help myself to plenty. Some plant their tiny saplings, some go for flowers. My mind is to breed bees for honey, although they say fresh milk from a cow is more profitable. My ambition is a white poodle dog and a coal black cat from the jungles and perhaps a little canary to wake me in the morning with a song, although with a cat in the house a canary might feel out of place . . . But I'll see about that in time. And then, with the help of God, I will find myself a wife. The women, I must tell you, are completely different there. Mostly blonde with blue eyes, humble, quiet and tender . . . one thing's sure: I myself will raise the children. I'll read them the stories and rock them to sleep at night with the songs my mother taught me . . . (*Drawing a picture for them*) Outside the snow storm rages, but inside the little house it is neat and warm. My wife is busy at the oven and I am rocking the baby.

(*Sings*)

ON A COLD AND FREEZING NIGHT
A LONELY CHILD COMES INTO SIGHT.
THE STARS LOOK DOWN FROM UP ON HIGH
AND WATCH THE STARVING CHILD GO BY.

GOD IN HEAVEN HEARS HIS SIGHS
SENDS AN ANGEL, DRIES HIS EYES,
SENDS A LITTLE CRUST OF BREAD
A LITTLE BED TO REST HIS HEAD.

Outside the storm rages. (*Imitates the storm*) My wife is busy at the oven preparing a thick, fat cabbage soup. I rock the baby.

(*Sings*)

LAST NIGHT YOU PROMISED ME ETERNAL
  LOVE
THIS MORNING YOU DISAPPEARED LIKE A
  FRIGHTENED DOVE.
I'M LEFT ALONE WITH ONE ETERNAL HOPE
TO SEE YOU SOME DAY HANGING FROM A
  ROPE.

(*There is a pause. The two policemen are stunned. Mechanically* PTAKH *throws away the butt of his cigarette. The* VAGABOND *goes after it*)

ACT I THE VAGABOND 19

PTAKH. Where are you going?
VAGABOND. (*Apologetically*) May I have the butt?
PTAKH. Go ahead . . .

(*As the* VAGABOND *picks up the butt* PTAKH *continues to* NIK)

Did you ever hear that . . . (*To* VAGABOND) Are you serious?
VAGABOND. (*Elegantly puffing*) Thank you.
NIK. But if what you're telling us is true . . .?
VAGABOND. So help me God. Siberia is larger than the rest of our country. More space, more air to breathe . . . For instance, take a river. Every dirty puddle here is called a river. In Siberia the rivers flow from the mountains like standing mirrors. And fish like you have never seen. For me there is no greater joy than fishing. Don't give me bread! Just let me sit at the water's edge with a fishing rod . . . I always make my own rod . . . (*He acts out the whole fishing experience*) I tear a long, thin branch from a tree . . . attach a long thread . . . a little worm . . . a tiny feather . . . "Clop" . . . in the water . . . Yes, brother, one has to know these things because it all depends on the casting. Some do it — (*Casting an imaginary line to one side*) "Whssssst" . . . Others do it — (*Casting to the other side*) "Plop" . . . I have my own way. Up and down — (*Casts up and down in front of him*) And a little fish is wriggling on the hook . . . Some seem to be made of silver, others of real gold, some have red noses, pink eyes, with blue tails. So help me God . . . And not all fish will be tempted by a miserable little worm . . . Each fish has its own palate. Some find flies tasty; others like a little frog, a sweet root, a juicy seed. Ah, brothers, you have to know all this . . . But when it comes to big fish — that is a completely different story . . . You can't catch a big fish with a little fishing rod. For

him you must have a net and you need muscle. This I lack. Because as you know I am of a delicate breed. Hard work is not for me . . . So what do I do? I hire a strong peasant. I give him five rubles and, "Pull, brother, pull" . . . and when he pulls the net out, if I find an eelpout, or a chub of some sort, I throw myself upon the fish as if he had pulled my own mother out of the water . . . Of course there are other problems . . . The eelpout and the pike are coarse fish. They'll grab anything, even a piece of wood. But when it comes to a bullhead, he will not touch anything but a butterfly. So what do I do? Off I go into the woods. And the woods there are deep and dark, with trees so tall that when you look up at them you get dizzy from the height. I catch a butterfly, attach a thread to its wings, crawl into the water, half naked and — "Clop" . . . Believe me, it's not as easy as it sounds because the roaring waters surge across the rocks and the currents can easily tear the slim threads . . . So you have to follow the butterfly as closely and as quietly as possible and that's not easy either. Sometimes you have to stand still for hours like a dead rock. (*Illustrating the dead rock*) And you think that's easy? Just try it — with the water bitter cold and your pants off! Sometimes you have to turn yourself into a tree so that the fish won't recognize your shadow under water. (*Illustrating a tree*) Get it? . . . Now, when it comes to a flounder — here's where you show what you're made of. You have to dive in — swim under water and do the catching with your hands. You hold your breath . . . here — it — comes — "Clop". (*Illustrates every step of the above*) That's Siberia for you, my friends! (*Pause. He sits down*) I wouldn't stay here if you paid me . . . (*Pointing*) The grey sky, the dirty drizzle that never stops, the heavy mist in the morning that creeps into your bones . . . But there! The great wide rivers . . . the high mountains . . . the thick forests . . .

the endless steppes ... (*Shouting*) "Ahooo — Ahooo —" At early dawn when the red reflection of the sun is first seen in the sky, I stand alone in the midst of a great plain as if I suddenly awoke in a huge bed with a white blanket of snow. The thousand-year-old trees watch me ... (*Screams*) Yes, brothers, they do watch me ... They shake their heads and mutter angrily, envious of that free little man as he stumbles over their roots, and climbs over the rocks up to the very top of the mountain. Without the slightest fear, either for my loneliness, or for the thunderous echo of my voice in that vast emptiness ... (*Calls again*) "Ahooo — Ahooo —" Such freedom, friends, you have never tasted. Perhaps many, many years ago your ancestors knew such freedom ... But you — how can I ever make you understand? How can I make you feel like you're standing on the topmost peak of the snow-capped mountain under the red reflection of the sun and shouting down, "Ahooooooo — Ahooooooo!"

(*Exhausted, he sits. They all sit in a heavy silence. Finally* PTAKH *takes to rolling a second cigarette*)

NIK. What you just told us only God in Heaven can understand. We poor people can't help it. We can't stop the rain falling from the sky, we cannot keep the road from filling up with mud ... (*Tearing off the sole of his boot and throwing it away*) All I can see is that my boot is of no use to me any longer and I'll have to finish the rest of the trip on one bare foot ... And when I come home there will be no kerosene in the lamp and my wife will be drunk.

PTAKH. Yes ... White mountains ... "Ahooooooo — Ahooooooo" ... Not for us, brother ... Nor is it for you! ... You will never reach those mountains. A man like me with strong feet might get there sometime, somehow. But a scarecrow like you —! You will fall apart like his boot in the middle of the road. You've only walked ten miles and look at you! Your nose has almost disappeared from your face.

NIK. And you still have thousands of miles to walk. We are only taking you to the next village. Then the others take care of you ... village after village ... town after town ... thousands of towns ... can you ever hope to cover them?

VAGABOND. Oh yes! I will. In every town, in every village there is, thank God, a police station with a resting room where they let me rest for a day or two. That's the law!

PTAKH. Resting room — in a basement where the filthy floor is crawling with all kinds of germs, thousands of towns, thousands of what you call resting rooms rotten with disease! ... A man must break down!

VAGABOND. I'll get there in spite of what you say!

PTAKH. But I say you can't!

VAGABOND. Yes I will!

PTAKH. (*Screaming violently*) Shut up, you lousy tramp! Have respect for your betters! When I say no — it's no!

(PTAKH *throws him across the Stage*)

NIK. He's right! You damn liar. (*Knocks* VAGABOND *over the head with the torn boot*) You forget that we are policemen! People of social standing and responsibility ... Show respect! ... Your silver mountains are not to be reached by ordinary feet in simple boots. Why do you say yes when we say no? (*In a tearful voice*) Why do you want to upset us? Just for spite?

PTAKH. And besides I don't believe a word he says! Why should I? Fish with red noses and gold tails. (*Laughs in hysterical despair*)

ACT I THE VAGABOND 23

NIK. Why should you lie to honest people?

PTAKH. We know those thieving black birds that come under the window crowing, "Ahooooooo, Ahooo, ahooo —" (*Slaps him in the rhythm of Ahooo*)

NIK. Even a thieving crow must have wings to get to those far unreachable mountains. We are people no matter how loud we crow, "Ahooo, ahooo — " We still remain where we belong. Sitting here on a broken tree, with a torn boot.

PTAKH. I could understand . . . on some good, two, three horses . . . on a train . . . but on your spindly legs . . . dead!

(*Both policemen scream through laughs and tears*)

PTAKH. (*Punches the* VAGABOND *in the stomach*) Dead!

VAGABOND. I'm sorry. You insisted I tell you my very truth. I'm sorry. I have no other truth. (*Pause*) I told you where I come from, but no one knows by what strange chances he will stop . . . when and where. All I can promise you is: if by some strange chance you happen to be in the neighborhood of the snowy mountains just look up and you'll hear my voice greeting you . . . "Ahooooooo . . . Ahooooooo . . ."

PTAKH. (*In furious rage*) Shut up I say, or I'll knock the guts out of you! (*Knocks him down to the ground*) Do you really think two poor decent men will drag themselves in the rain and mud so that you should be able to sing a baby to sleep? No, brother! Forget the "Ahooooo . . . Ahoooo." You'll die on the road! But if you should happen to survive they'll send you for hard labor anyway, even in Siberia. And while you're working your wife will be lying in bed with a carpenter! . . . And if we should ever meet again you'll thank us for a drop of water, for a crumb of bread, or the butt of my cigarette. You goddamn liar! Here, take it!

(*He throws the butt on the ground. All three sit for a while sunk in their own thoughts*)

NIK. (*Stands*) Well, time to go . . . We've rested long enough.

(*Slowly and melancholically, he limps Offstage.* PTAKH *follows him gloomily, stops, gestures to the* VAGA-BOND *to follow him, and walks Offstage. The* VAGABOND, *after a moment, gets up slowly, wipes the blood off his nose and face, picks up the butt, inhales with relish, puts his collar up, puts hands crossways in his sleeves and follows them Offstage proudly.*)

(THE CURTAIN FALLS)

II

THE WITCH

Characters:

RAISA

SAVELY

THE POSTMAN

A small log cabin which adjoins a little church, somewhere in the snowy parts of the Russian countryside. The panes of the only window are covered with frost. We can hear the howling of a fierce snow storm outside. Right of the window, a shelf with a few earthenware plates and cups, and a tea kettle. Near the window, a broom and some kindling wood. In the center of the room a small wooden table with 2-3 small benches at the sides. A kerosene lamp on the table with a shade improvised from an old strip of paper. On the right there is a double couch-bed. Over it in the corner hangs a triptych icon.

On the left side there's an old-fashioned stove with an opening close to the floor with a fire burning in it. The entrance left leads through a half visible antechamber to the outside. In that corner there are steps leading up to the belfry, where two ropes are hanging down from the invisible bells. To the side of the belfry — perhaps as a backdrop — are the tops of two or three long, colored windows of a church. SAVELY, *the deacon of the church, lies huddled on the couch-bed covered with a heavy, old blanket with patches pulled up over his head.* RAISA, *his wife, is sitting on one of the small benches facing the oven. She is patching up a couple of blankets. She is a corpulent, good-looking woman, bursting with femininity. Several times she turns to the window listening to the howling winds. Suddenly she strains her body listening intently to a far, hardly-audible ringing of horse bells. In order not to awaken her husband, she goes on tiptoe to look out the window, rubs the ice off the glass, and as the bells fade out she returns to her place busying herself by stoking the fire in the oven. After a while the jingling of the bells seems to come closer. She rushes again to the window.* SAVELY *suddenly creeps out from under the blanket. They look at each other meaningfully.*

SAVELY *is a pug-nosed man of indistinguishable age. He has fading red hair which is (in the traditional style of Russian clerics) combed back into a short pigtail.*

SAVELY. (*In a hollow, tearful voice*) I know . . . I know everything.

(*There is no response from* RAISA *except a look of disgust*)

SAVELY. (*Continued*) Why don't you come to bed?
RAISA. I have work to do.
SAVELY. It's late.
RAISA. On a night like this I have to keep the oven warm, don't I? Go to sleep. Don't bother me.

(SAVELY *covers his head with the blanket. As the raging wind outside subsides, the jingling of the bells becomes more clear.* RAISA, *holding the cover she works on, races to the window*)

SAVELY. (*Emerging from under the blanket*) What are you doing?

RAISA. On a night like this we need more covers.

SAVELY. Then why did you plaster your nose to the window?

RAISA. Now don't start with that again. We had enough of that. Sleep I say! (*She goes back to the bench*)

SAVELY. What are you looking for?

RAISA. To see the snow falling, you damn, darn fool.

SAVELY. I thought I heard bells ringing outside. (*As he rises to his knees on the bed with his hand to his ear*) Eh — sounds like bells all right.

RAISA. (*Picks up her sewing*) It is probably the postman's sleigh on the way to the railroad station.

SAVELY. How do you know?

RAISA. I didn't say I know, I said: "Probably". In weather like this the postman always puts a collar with bells around the horse's neck, doesn't he?

SAVELY. The postman died more than a month ago already . . .

RAISA. So what? The post office remained . . . Letters are taken to the railroad station . . . aren't they?

SAVELY. In weather like this people should not write any letters.

RAISA. Why don't you stop them, you darn fool.

SAVELY. In weather like this, nobody should be out, not even a mangy dog.

RAISA. The postman is a government official — he's got to be on the job whether he likes it or not.

SAVELY. Keep your mouth shut! . . . sha — sh — (*He listens intently, crosses himself*) Blessed be God . . .

He's gone. (*He covers himself with his blanket; the bells start jingling again. He jumps up*) Back again.

(*She ignores him, goes to pick up a plaid for the cover she's working on. He slips off the couch and stares out the window, then turns to* RAISA)

SAVELY. (*Continued*) Seems to be going round and round in circles . . .

RAISA. No wonder. With no moon in the sky on a night like this . . .

SAVELY. Then why have you swept the moon off the sky?

RAISA. You crazy nut.

SAVELY. Don't tell me what a witch can do . . .

RAISA. You really think I have the moon in my pocket?

SAVELY. Chasing the poor postman around not letting him go where he is supposed to . . .

RAISA. Are you going to have one of your fits again tonight . . .

SAVELY. From the first day I married you I knew you were not what you seemed to be . . .

RAISA. Bite your tongue you ugly snake. (*Crosses herself*)

SAVELY. If I ever turn into a snake it will be your work. As it is written in the Holy Scripture: no man can protect himself from the witchcraft of a witch like you.

RAISA. If you say it once again, I'll go right through the storm to the Holy Father Nikodim and tell him all about your blasphemous talk under the roof of a church.

SAVELY. I am a deacon of the church . . . a servant of God . . . and must abide by the commandment: you shall not permit or even tolerate any sort of witchery in the house of God.

RAISA. The Holy Father will chase you out as once before.

SAVELY. He doesn't know ... But I know everything. In the late autumn there were heavy showers for three days and nights ... remember?

RAISA. Remember what?

SAVELY. The man who came knocking at our door.

RAISA. He was a friend of my father.

SAVELY. Didn't he know your father died long ago? ... Then what did he come for?

RAISA. He couldn't find his way, all the roads were under water.

SAVELY. So was our road. How did he manage to find the way under water to our door?

RAISA. In distress people look for any roof or door. Don't people jump to save a drowning dog?

SAVELY. But did you ever hear a dog giggle all night long? What were you giggling about so much all night long?

RAISA. Nobody was giggling, we were sitting at the table hardly talking to each other ... Just listening to the way you were snoring all night long.

SAVELY. You thought I was asleep, but I heard everything under my blanket.

RAISA. You disgusting liar. You must have been dreaming.

SAVELY. And in the early morning when he left he had black rings under his eyes and his cheeks were sunken in too. Why? See? I know everything.

RAISA. You know nothing. (*She turns to stoke the fire in the oven*)

SAVELY. And then again last winter a sudden freezing cold turned all the roads of the valley into one white sheet of glass ... and sure enough another giggling dog found his way to our door.

RAISA. What kind of stories are you making up? That was the sheriff of the village near Kolino.

SAVELY. A sheriff should know better than to molest people in the middle of the night. A sheriff should know all the roads of his territory in a blizzard or even in a deluge.

RAISA. His hands and legs were frozen. The poor man was practically a frozen corpse.

SAVELY. But the corpse knew how to find his way here all right!

RAISA. He didn't take up much room here. He slept right there in the corner, on the floor.

SAVELY. But the whole night the frozen corpse kept twisting, turning and groaning on the floor . . . I never heard a corpse doing that . . . See — you are blushing . . . Red in the face . . . like a lobster.

RAISA. (*Turning her back*) Did you ever see yourself in a mirror you old creep?

SAVELY. Why did you blow the lamp out?

RAISA. To save the kerosene you fool, don't we always do?

SAVELY. I tell you, I saw everything.

RAISA. You saw nothing . . . there was nothing there to see.

SAVELY. The winter wasn't over yet and another frozen corpse showed up.

RAISA. (*With a smile*) My God, you're bringing up that police commissioner again? . . .

SAVELY. That's right. You spread your arms, "Come in, come in, my dear man."

RAISA. He was an important man, wasn't he?

SAVELY. He was an ugly fellow with a flat nose, a face full of pimples and a twisted neck into the bargain. Why you should ever have bothered to shake up a blizzard over a horrible-looking animal like that I will never understand.

ACT II THE WITCH 31

(*The jingling of the bells becomes louder*)

SAVELY. (*Continued*) There they are again . . . the jingling of the devil.

(RAISA *snatches the lamp from the table, races to the window and starts to signal with it*)

SAVELY. (*Continued*) May I be struck dead if I let you have your way again. (*Tries to pull the lamp from her hands*) There is a church behind this wall and I will not permit any more of these goings on here. This is sacred ground . . . I am a man of God.

(*They are fighting to grab the lamp from each other*)

RAISA. A man of God with no pity in his heart. (*She gives up the lamp*) Oh, let the poor postman freeze to death. What is that to me . . . If anything, you'll have to answer to the Holy Father Nikodim . . .

SAVELY. (*Puts the lamp back on the table*) Well then, why don't you put an end to the storm? Say one of your diabolic curses and stop it . . .

RAISA. I should stop the storm?

SAVELY. You started it, you stop it!

RAISA. You are out of your mind.

SAVELY. You will be whirling and twirling the winds into the snow until you push the postman right into the house . . .

RAISA. If you say it once again, I'll throw the lamp in your face . . . What do you want of me?

SAVELY. A long time ago I realized that every time you get restless, filled with anger, cursing nature, the wind starts to wail behind the window, a gale begins to blow with the icy breath of a thousand demons and all roads get lost . . . except the one that leads to our door . . . And here they come—the devils in disguise of frozen corpses. (*He goes to the bed*)

RAISA. They come to see you, not me.

SAVELY. They won't come here tonight . . . the bells are gone. (*He crosses himself*) If you were not a witch, you would be more careful with those evil spirits in disguise.

RAISA. Go on, cross yourself, you old fool! You are a demon with a pigtail . . . When my father was the priest in this church, anybody could stop by to rest and pray . . . But now, if a man stops to warm up a little, you see nothing but a devil in disguise.

SAVELY. Why don't women ever stop here? Do only men ever lose their way in a blizzard? . . . If they would stop here for a drink of water or even for a bite of bread and leave, I wouldn't mind. But do they have to stay all night and giggle? (*He lies down*)

(*The jingling of the bells comes again but clearer*)

SAVELY. (*Continued*) Eh — eh — don't move, don't move, I said . . . He may pass again.

(*She leaves her seat and is about to pick up the lamp again*)

SAVELY. (*Continued*) Oh no, not this time, sister. I knew this morning that you were working up a storm for tonight.

(*She breaks away from the table, rushes up the steps to the belfry, grips the ropes of the church bells and pulls violently. The roar of the wind and the sound of the bells mingle in a ferocious din. SAVELY follows her up and struggles with her for the ropes.*

ACT II THE WITCH

She drops one and grabs the other. He follows her)

RAISA. Let go! Let go, I say.

SAVELY. (*Fighting*) I must not allow a witch to touch the bells of a church.

RAISA. You are hurting me! Your fingers are like the teeth of a hyena!

(*He succeeds in tearing the ropes out of her grip. She comes down into the room. The bells continue to ring by inertia*)

RAISA. (*Continued*) Oh, let him get lost in the snow for all I care.

SAVELY. (*Following her down*) I warn you for the last time . . . If you succeed in blowing another visitor in here tonight, the first thing in the morning I'll go to Father Nikodim . . .

RAISA. (*Wildly*) Go ahead! Who's stopping you?

SAVELY. I'll go and report in detail what's going on in my house . . .

RAISA. He'll put you where you belong. In the crazy house.

SAVELY. "Father," I'll say, "my wife is a witch. You want to know what, why, and how? . . . Come, Your Holiness, and see with your own eyes mighty sinful tricks she's performing . . . Doing this and that and many other things . . . See with your own eyes."

RAISA. Let him come. He can't do a thing to me. This house belongs to me by the will of my father.

SAVELY. Father Nikodim will send you to eternal damnation in hell where you will broil on hot coals with Satan's children dancing around you . . .

(*In the distance, knocking is heard on the door of the church. Man and wife remain still for a moment.*

The knocking is repeated. The POSTMAN'S *voice is heard from far outside)*

POSTMAN. Is anybody there? . . . For the love of God, let me in! Hey! Good people, open the door! I've lost my way! I'm freezing out here!
RAISA. (*In a loud voice*) Who is it?
POSTMAN. The postman . . . I'm on the way to the train-station in Pontok with the mail . . .
RAISA. The postman!
SAVELY. I knew you would do it again . . .

(RAISA *grabs her heavy cover*)

SAVELY. (*Continued*) Stay here, I said. I am going to the Holy Father this minute. I will bring him here . . .

(*He is looking for his boots.* RAISA *goes through the opening of the antechamber. One can hear her open the door-bar. Roar of the wind is heard.*)

RAISA'S VOICE. (*Offstage*) The church is closed. Here's the door, around the corner.
SAVELY. (*Continued*) Stop it! Stop it, I'm warning you!

(*In helpless frustration he scurries toward the bed and, whimpering, huddles up under the blanket. After a few fitful kicks he remains quiet. We hear voices from outside mixed with the roaring of the wind*)

POSTMAN. (*Entering antechamber*) Thank you! Thank you good woman! What a night! I have never been in one like this before.
RAISA. You'd better tie the horse to the stump . . .

ACT II   THE WITCH   35

POSTMAN. The horse hardly moves, he's a crusted piece of ice . . . poor beast.

(*As* RAISA *moves into the room she's followed by a tall man in boots. He wears a black coat with two rows of metal buttons, a grey fur cap and heavy gloves. He's completely covered with snow. As he takes his cap off a young, blondish peasant is discovered*)

POSTMAN. (*Continued*) I heard some church bells . . . was that a church door I was knocking at? (*Looks around*)
RAISA. Used to be.
POSTMAN. I tried to force it open . . . I am sorry. If not for the bells — I'd be really lost. I passed this place several times 'round and 'round . . . I saw a flicker from a light . . . but when I turned toward it I was again where I was before . . . near the locked door. How can you know where you are when there is just a white wall before your eyes . . . whichever way you turn . . .
RAISA. We tried with our lamp . . .
POSTMAN. You say we . . . (*Turns to bed*) Is someone sleeping here?
RAISA. That's my husband. . . . Comes this time of night he is very much asleep.
POSTMAN. I'm really sorry. I wouldn't bother you but I think I got frost-bite in my toes. (*Knocks his legs against each other, pulls his heavy gloves off, rubs his hands, shakes the snow off his body*) The howling wind spits into your eyes . . . blinds you . . . most of the time I couldn't see further than my nose . . . once or twice the horse and sleigh were almost lifted up and turned around . . . If not for your spark of light I wouldn't know there was any life around here at all. When I

heard the bells I turned back . . . but no matter which way I turned there was just the same white wall in front of me . . . Where in God's name am I now?

RAISA. This is the back room of a small church . . . (*She points to belfry*)

POSTMAN. Is it far from Kolino?

RAISA. You're ten miles off the main road . . .

POSTMAN. Ten miles! Christ! How could I have gotten off the road so far?

(*The wind slams the front door in the antechamber*)

RAISA. Let me lock the door before the wind tears it off.

POSTMAN. Wait, wait. I think I'd better pull in the mail sacks for a while . . . the mail must be soaked by now.

RAISA. That's right. The letters may be ruined if you leave them out in the sleigh much longer. (*She covers him with a quilt she worked on*)

POSTMAN. There may be some important official letters and I am responsible for every single letter.

RAISA. You might as well bring them in and try to dry them out by the stove.

(*He strides out.* RAISA *gets busy, stirs up the fire in the oven . . .* SAVELY *pops out from underneath the blanket*)

SAVELY. (*Shaking his finger at her*) Tomorrow I go to the Holy Father . . .

RAISA. Didn't you hear he has frost-bite in his legs.

SAVELY. I'm warning you. One postman was put behind bars for ten years for one single letter. For a whole pack he may be sent to Siberia for life and the weather there is even worse than here.

ACT II THE WITCH 37

(*As* POSTMAN *brings in two sacks,* SAVELY *crawls quickly under cover like a turtle back into his shell. The front door slams,* RAISA *rushes to secure the door.* POSTMAN *shakes snow off his pack, rubs his hands near the oven.* RAISA *comes back*)

RAISA. A nice glass of hot tea would thaw you out a little.

POSTMAN. Ten miles out of the way! I'll be damned. I might miss the train altogether. I wish I knew what time it was.

RAISA. We have no clock. But in the morning when the sun is up, I can tell the time to the minute.

POSTMAN. I am new on the job and don't know much about these parts . . .

RAISA. I wouldn't try to find the road on a night like this.

POSTMAN. I am from the South . . . thought I'd get into civil service here. There are good chances for promotion . . . But it's not an easy start. The change of weather here is mighty rough. A snowy desert with no signs . . . I even let my nag feel my anger with a couple of lashes over his ass. I wish I could do something for the poor beast but . . . I can't very well bring him in and put him on the stove.

(*Both laugh*)

RAISA. Don't worry. I'll cover him up with this warm blanket. You'd better take your boots off. Frost-bite is no joke.

POSTMAN. (*Sits down*) It's not an easy thing when your feet swell up.

RAISA. (*Takes off her large apron*) We'll do it . . . the way the men do. Stretch your legs. (*Takes his foot between her legs and pulls*)

POSTMAN. I really can't spare the time for this.

RAISA. Don't be lazy . . . push! (*She pulls off the boot*) You just get the chill out of your bones and you'll move on. (*She takes off second boot*) Now you'll put your feet by the stove.

POSTMAN. (*As if noticing her for the first time*) You're a good woman. What are you doing in a place like this?

RAISA. We are part of the old church here. My husband and I . . . He is there . . . Hey, Savely, get up! We have a visitor.

(*There is no reply*)

RAISA. (*Continued*) It's been some time since anyone passed here. People used to stop by . . . to visit the church. But since they opened the main road, nobody comes this way anymore . . . and there's nothing much left of the church . . . except the bells . . . One for weekends, one for Christmas. (*She serves him tea*) There is plenty of black bread. If you prefer a piece of white, or perhaps a baked potato . . . (*She wipes sweat from forehead*) My husband is the deacon. He watches over what's left of the church (*She wipes her forehead and opens her blouse a little*)

POSTMAN. (*While drinking the tea*) What is there to watch? Who would carry the church bells off?

RAISA. That's true . . . Nobody comes here anyway.

POSTMAN. Then why don't you move somewhere else?

RAISA. He wants to stay here and I am his wife. He's sort of shy with people — and as long as there is a deacon, they will keep the church.

POSTMAN. (*In good humor*) What good is a church without people to pray in it?

RAISA. There is a little scrap of land in the back. We

ACT II   THE WITCH   39

plant in the spring and store up food for the winter. But lately the Holy Father Nikodim claims that this piece of land belongs to the new church built in the center of Kolino . . . and there is nobody to help us.

(SAVELY *leaps from under the cover screeching furiously*)

SAVELY. That is a wicked lie. Father Nikodim is a saintly man. He knows what he is doing. (*Pointing his finger at the* POSTMAN) And you keep your frozen nose out of this. If you want to keep your soul out of hell . . . get out of here! Get out! (*Out of breath, he scurries under the blanket again*)

POSTMAN. (*Not much disturbed, smiles*) He doesn't seem very hospitable, your husband . . . Have you been married long?

RAISA. (*Wiping her sweat, busy serving*) Four years next autumn . . . My father used to be the deacon here. When he fell ill, they didn't bother to wait until he died—they sent a new man to replace him. My poor father was so worried about the piece of land back there—behind the church . . . he felt if I married the new deacon we could at least keep that . . . so . . . here I am . . .

POSTMAN. It seems your husband killed *three* birds with one shot . . . A job, a wife, and a piece of land at the same time. Some people have all the luck.

(*The storm is heard as a violent roar outside*)

POSTMAN. (*Continued*) Sounds like all hell broke loose.

RAISA. (*Wipes the sweat from her brow, loosens her collar*) I'm sure it's going to keep up like that all night . . . and it's nice and warm here. Perhaps another glass of tea . . .

POSTMAN. It makes me drowsy . . .

40   THE WITCH   ACT II

RAISA. Maybe you ought to have a little nap before you try again. I could spread this in the corner on the floor. (*She starts to arrange the plaids that she has been sewing on the floor in front of the oven*)

POSTMAN. The floor is as good a place as any.

RAISA. I'll lay out a few of these for a pillow.

POSTMAN. Just a wink or two . . . I must move on.

RAISA. (*As she arranges the bedding on her knees*) It's nice and warm here.

POSTMAN. It sure is. But the train won't wait . . . the mail must be delivered on time . . . I may lose my job.

(*After an awkward pause, they look at each other. He lies down. Strong wind roaring*)

POSTMAN. (*Continued*) Hope the wind doesn't pull the chimney off. (*Stretches out yawning. Closes his eyes and mumbles*) A real war in the air . . . winds fighting winds, mother nature screaming murder . . .

(RAISA *unfastens her skirt in the back. It falls to the floor. She sits on the stool and watches him*)

SAVELY. (*Moves restlessly under the blanket, sticks his head out*) What are you doing there?

RAISA. (*In a hoarse voice*) Don't bother . . . He's tired and fell asleep.

(SAVELY *jumps off the bed, rushes to the sleeping* POSTMAN *and covers his face with the blanket*)

RAISA. (*Continued*) What are you doing that for?

SAVELY. The light is too much in his eyes.

RAISA. Then put the light out . . .

(*As she is about to do so, he grabs her hand at the lamp*)

THE WITCH

SAVELY. Aha . . . So you are a witch!

RAISA. You red-headed scarecrow. Why can't you leave him alone for a while.

SAVELY. A man should not sleep on the floor . . . He will get a stiff neck. Hey, you get up! You will get a stiff neck.

RAISA. Leave him alone! Can't you see the man's frozen dead? He needs a rest.

SAVELY. Dead or alive, he's on a government job and not supposed to sleep while on duty . . . Hey, you, get up! (*Kicks the* POSTMAN *with his foot*) Get up! Or I'll report you! What is your name? (*Kicks him again, stumbles and falls on top of the* POSTMAN)

RAISA. Get off him this minute! Leave the poor man alone!

(*She grabs* SAVELY *and throws him aside. The* POSTMAN *sits up*)

SAVELY. People are waiting for letters and he's loafing around here. (*To* POSTMAN *on floor*) You ought to be ashamed of yourself. The train is not going to wait for you, I tell you. You'd better get up. I'll show you the way to the station. I'll just put my boots on.

(*He scampers toward the bed and pulls the boots out from under it. The* POSTMAN, *sitting on the floor, seems befuddled and drops back onto the floor.* SNAVELY *already has his boots on and goes to the* POSTMAN *again*)

SAVELY. (*Continued*) The storm is almost over.

RAISA. You damn liar . . .

SAVELY. (*To* POSTMAN) Are you deaf? Can't you hear the train whistling? They may be calling for you.

RAISA. How would you know?

SAVELY. Keep your mouth shut. Are you the postman or is he the postman? Eh? If he has to go, let him go . . . And if he doesn't want to go . . . he has to go anyway. (*Gets his coat and high hat*)

RAISA. How can you push a man out into this cold? And the horse is frozen and can't move . . .

SAVELY. Never mind. I'll cover the horse with my blanket. In a minute he'll be alright. (*Is about to take the cover off the bed*)

RAISA. (*Jumps on bed*) The blanket is mine. (*Grabs the cover*)

SAVELY. (*Tugging with her*) And what about the horse? Who's going to deliver the mail? The world is waiting for letters. People's lives may depend on him. Just because you want to play with wind and storm . . . stop playing with the devil you shameless witch.

(*She yanks the blanket away from him. The* POSTMAN *stirs*)

POSTMAN. What in hell is going on here?

SAVELY. The train is waiting . . . Come, I will show you the road to the station.

RAISA. The train is gone by now . . .

SAVELY. You can still make it, I tell you. Come, I will show you the road.

(*While* RAISA *is covering the bed,* SAVELY *takes the large church keys off a hook on the wall, unnoticed by the others. He then takes the mail sacks and carries them out of the house. She runs after him, closes the door-bar, comes back triumphantly*)

POSTMAN. (*Sits up, stretches*) I feel as though all my bones are broken . . . I could use a few more minutes of rest . . .

RAISA. Why not? Why not?

(*He gets up*)

RAISA. (*Continued*) I have closed the door . . . Look, I have to tell you something . . . Have another glass of tea.

POSTMAN. Even if I missed the train, it sure would do me good to show myself at the station. (*He puts his boots on*)

RAISA. Every two, three days there's another train . . . Good Lord, why drag yourself out in this awful night! Look, the door is closed . . . with the bar.

POSTMAN. (*Looks at her*) You're a good woman . . . Good-looking too. What's your name?

RAISA. Raisa.

POSTMAN. Nice . . . I like the name.

RAISA. (*Lowering her eyes*) Just a little while . . .

POSTMAN. (*Innocently*) I'd like to . . . But I can't . . .

RAISA. Another glass of tea . . . and I closed the door.

POSTMAN. What a beautiful neck you have . . . and shoulders . . . (*Places his hand on her shoulder*) You feel so soft . . . You're a good-looking woman.

RAISA. Then why don't you stay.

POSTMAN. I don't think your husband cares for me much . . .

RAISA. He doesn't care much for anybody. So why should you worry? It won't take long to boil the water . . . I closed the door with the bar.

SAVELY. (*Knocks at the door*) Come on, hurry up! Your horse is frozen stiff! Looks like a snow horse. Don't you have any pity for the poor animal? Come on!

(*His voice gets lost in a new roar of the storm*)

RAISA. You hear . . . The storm is getting worse . . . I know what I am talking about.

POSTMAN. (*After a slight pause*) You're so nice . . . and strong.

RAISA. So what are you afraid of? The door is locked.

(*For a minute they look into each other's eyes. Suddenly he embraces her passionately. As she sinks onto the edge of the bed he begins to unbutton his coat.* SAVELY *appears at the belfry and begins to ring the bells. The pair remain petrified in their positions while* SAVELY *leaves the bells ringing and comes down into the room*)

SAVELY. You didn't think I had a key to the church door? I'm still the deacon here. I put the mail back in the sleigh. I'll show you which way will bring you to the station.

POSTMAN. (*Regaining his composure, he crosses himself, puts on his coat*) Well, that's that . . . I guess I'd better go . . . (*Hearing sleigh bells, he rushes to the window*) What happened to the beast?

SAVELY. The animal would have died, I tell you . . . he's got to move to keep alive . . . so I let him move around . . .

POSTMAN. (*Grabbing him with sudden rage*) Hey you . . . get going! Come on! And you'd better show me the way to the road like you said . . .!

(*He pushes* SAVELY *forward.* SAVELY *turns back the bar of the door and they walk out.* RAISA *rushes to the door, cries out into the night and is slammed back by a violent gust of wind. She climbs up to the belfry and wildly pulls the ropes throwing the church bells into a frightful dissonance. She goes into a wild rage breaking some earthen jars, benches, kettles, etc. Exhausted, she falls on the*

ACT II THE WITCH 45

bed crying hysterically. When the bells and the woman's weeping subside, SAVELY *returns. He's out of breath, wrapped in the cover he took for the horse. He believes* RAISA *is asleep and tries not to make much noise as he shakes off the snow*)

SAVELY. (*While taking off his coat*) I'm sorry. It just didn't work this time . . . God in heaven heard the bells . . . Just the same, the first thing in the morning I'll go to His Holiness Father Nikodim and tell him what sort of wife I am cursed with.

RAISA. (*In a fury*) Go! Go to Father Nikodim! If you drop dead I would not miss you! You better go first thing in the morning and find yourself another wife, you creeping spider!

SAVELY. I'm sorry . . . ! I snatched the bone right out from between your teeth!

RAISA. Why did you come back! Why couldn't you get lost, or be swept away by the storm, or hit by a falling tree? Why couldn't you get swallowed up by the darkness, you toothless hyena? I could have been a good wife to anyone but you! Why didn't he put you on the train with his mail and send you straight to hell? Why didn't he do it, that ungrateful jackass! . . .

(*As she buries her face in the pillow a great burst of wind hits the window*)

SAVELY. Here it comes again . . . Still trying your tricks . . . Your blood didn't stop boiling yet. Well, you'd better calm down. It won't do you any good tonight any more. Calm down and go to sleep. No use trying any more I tell you . . .

(*He drops his boots and his coat, braces himself, and crawls across her on the bed. He listens for a while to the sudden calmness. Then, hesitating, touches her head and caresses her braids. He tickles his nose once or twice with one of her braids. A faint wind laments outside the window as the curtain falls*)

III

IN A MUSIC SHOP

Characters:

SHOPKEEPER

IVAN

A bright, hot, summer day. A music shop in a provincial town. There are shelves with music sheets. A few old musical instruments are on display in the window. Near the door is a little stand with a flower pot on it. Behind the counter is the SHOPKEEPER, a good-natured, heavy-set, simple man.

A cat lies sleeping on the counter. The bell over the door rings. IVAN, *a perspiring, elderly gentleman, loaded with many large and small packages, enters.*

IVAN. (*Loses a small package. Bends to pick it up*) Good morning . . . Excuse me . . .

SHOPKEEPER. Good morning! Good morning, sir!

IVAN. What a day! I feel like a roasted chicken! . . . Excuse me . . . Could I get the music of the . . . I wonder . . . Do you have the music of . . . I mean . . . Would you be kind enough to let me have the music of . . . How much does it cost?

SHOPKEEPER. What music do you want? Vocal, piano, symphonic . . .? We have a big stock, but you have to tell me exactly what piece you're looking for.

IVAN. Of course. I know that . . . That's what I'm trying to tell you . . . I'd like to have the piano music . . . the piano . . . I mean not the piano but the music.

SHOPKEEPER. What music?

IVAN. The music of . . . Oh curse it! What a day! I feel I'm just melting away . . . and ready to drop like an overloaded horse . . . Would you be kind enough to let me put my packages down for a moment? Since early morning I've been running around like a chicken with its head chopped off . . . buying this, buying that . . . not a thing for myself. All these packages are for my wife and there is no end to what that woman needs . . . There is nothing she can't use . . . And I'm her errand boy. Oh, yes, that's exactly what I am! . . . Her errand boy. So . . . would you be good enough to let me have the music of . . . Oh heck! What in the world is the name of it? The music . . . you know it . . .

SHOPKEEPER. I don't . . .

IVAN. Please, don't say that . . . How is it possible? It's very popular. Everybody knows it, everybody sings it, plays it . . . I just happened to forget the name of it.

SHOPKEEPER. Oh, the name! I've got plenty of names. (*Quickly takes stack of old music sheets. Reads names*) "To My Dear Mother's Day", "My Lost Baby", "God Bless You, My Beloved", "We Entered Paradise Together."

IVAN. No, no. It's something entirely different . . . It's more delicate, more refined . . . more . . . You see, I almost have it on the tips of my fingers, but I can't catch on to it . . . How do you like that!

SHOPKEEPER. I have plenty of music. I'm sure it's here . . .

IVAN. Oh, I'm sure you have it. What music shop doesn't? It's very popular . . . But it just slipped my mind completely. As I opened your door I had it right

ACT III　　IN A MUSIC SHOP　　49

on the tip of my tongue. I was about to say, "Will you please give me the music of . . ." And in the same breath it was gone. How is it possible? I was right here on the threshold clearing my throat to say, politely, simply, calmly, "Have you got the music of . . .?" And in that split second it fell off my tongue and was lost on the floor like a rolling coin.

SHOPKEEPER. Well, I'm afraid you won't find it on the floor.

IVAN. Naturally! That was just a figure of speech.

SHOPKEEPER. You say when you opened the door you wanted to ask for it? Are you positive that you remembered it before you walked in?

IVAN. Absolutely. But you see, now I'm a bit confused . . . I'm not sure whether I don't remember what I forgot or I forgot what I don't remember . . . As I crossed the street I said to myself, "Ah — ah — ah — here is the music shop. Go in and ask for . . ." God in Heaven! I pleaded with her . . . that is, with my wife . . . On my knees I begged her, "Please, write it down on a piece of paper!" But she: "No, no, no . . ." I ask you, why couldn't she put it down on a little scrap of paper?

SHOPKEEPER. How should I know? How could I know?

IVAN. Why do you keep on telling me, "No, no, no"? Who should know but you? . . . You are a man of music and all I'm talking about is in relation to music, no?

SHOPKEEPER. What music?

IVAN. That's what I don't remember! A man of my age can't keep everything in his head . . . After all, it's one little bit of a head for so many names of things, packages . . . places . . . prices . . . How could I? . . . So I thought, maybe . . . perhaps . . . somehow . . . in some way . . . you could guess, or at least help me to remember the music I was supposed to get . . . You can't, eh?

SHOPKEEPER. Well, it depends a lot on the type of music . . . For instance, can you recall any part of the melody?

IVAN. The melody is not too complicated. As a matter of fact, it's quite simple . . . It starts like, "Ah-ah-ah . . . ah-ah-ah . . ." Then it sort of turns around a little, "Ta-ta-ta . . . " Eh? . . . No? . . . You don't know it?

SHOPKEEPER. Look here, my dear sir . . . half of the music on these shelves starts with, "Ah, ah, ah, ah" and then turns around to, "Ta, ta, ta, ta".

IVAN. All right. All right. It's not necessary to explain that. I'm not a baby! . . . I definitely remember . . . It starts, "Ta, ta, ta, tata," but where it goes from there, I can't remember.

SHOPKEEPER. If you don't remember the melody or the name, how do you expect me to help you?

IVAN. Well then, what shall I do? . . . I can't go home without the music. She'll eat me up alive . . . You see, Clara . . . that is, my wife . . . she's a singer . . . She may not be exactly a singer in the true sense of the word, but she likes to sing. When she gets the urge to sing, there's no way of stopping her. All day long . . . like a bird . . . from early morning 'til late at night, like a little bird . . . Of course, this is also a figure of speech. There is nothing about her that could make one mistake her for a little bird. She's rather a tall woman . . . Quite well developed, especially in the front, which is, as they say, to the advantage of a singer, but don't worry, there is plenty of her in the back . . . front, sides . . . all around . . . I'd say she's a bit on the heavy side. Between you and me, a little too heavy for my taste . . . But, thank God, she's always in the best of health . . . Never a headache . . . not even a toothache . . . But a voice! A voice she has! You may not like her singing, but as for volume . . . why, you can hear her for miles around . . . And God forbid you should suggest a little pianissimo, you're liable to get slapped, right, left. As I said, she's a fairly strong, corpulent woman ... and a temper ... Eh-eh! (*Turns the exclamation into a melody:*) Eh! Eh! Eh! ... Nothing, eh?

(SHOPKEEPER *shakes his head.* IVAN *dejectedly continues*)

IVAN. (*Continued*) Well then, what is to be done? If I come home without the music, there'll be the devil to pay. She gets furious and in such a state she can't always control herself ... She just lets herself go ... right, left ... smack, smack!

SHOPKEEPER. (*Sympathetically*) I see, I see ... But why not concentrate on more positive things? For instance, can you go back and remember what she told you when you left the house?

IVAN. Of course I remember. She distinctly said, "Take the local train and when you arrive in the city buy this ... buy that ... buy that ... buy this ... and then rush to the music shop and get me the mu ..." mu ... now come on! Come on! Help a little! What's the matter with you? ... Just standing, looking at me! (*Breaks into a laugh*) What a beautiful cat you have ... (*Patting the sleeping cat on the counter*) Kitty, kitty, kitty ... meow.

(*Cat hisses,* IVAN *recoils*)

IVAN. (*Continued*) Who do you think you are? Lolling around in the sun all day long. I'm sure there are plenty of mice having a good time right under your nose, but you are just lazying around here. Meow ... (*Turns to* SHOPKEEPER) By the way, what is she? A him or a her?

SHOPKEEPER. She's a he.

IVAN. I should say so! No *she* ever had such a gorgeous mustache. (*Touches cat*) Meow ... Ahhh, you're no good. You're just a lazy loafer of a pussy cat. That's what you are. Other cats are out now doing their daily work . . . sweating out their daily bread and butter . . . but you are just lying, licking, curling your mustache . . . meow . . . meow . . . (*Suddenly turns to* SHOPKEEPER, *sings:*) meow . . . meow . . . meow . . . Nothing . . . Eh?

(SHOPKEEPER *silently shakes his head*)

IVAN. (*Continued*) Well, that's that. So I'll take my things and go home. (*Takes his hat*) One thing's for sure. You have a nice, good-looking cat . . . which makes me think . . . what about kittens? If you have some kittens I'll take one off your hands.

SHOPKEEPER. I told you, it's not a she, but a he.

IVAN. Oh yes, that's right. I'm sorry. What a pity. You see my wife is actually crazy about cats. So, if I brought her a little kitten it might make her forget the music for a while . . . or at least keep her temper down. Don't you think so? Well, what do you say?

SHOPKEEPER. All I know is there is no pet shop in this neighborhood. Perhaps the best thing for you would be to tell the truth . . . I could be a witness.

IVAN. You mean instead of a kitten I should bring you home? That would be something! I wouldn't wish it on my worst enemy . . . She would let herself go . . . Slap, slap, right, left.

SHOPKEEPER. Please, calm yourself . . . A word or two from a stranger may help. She may understand.

IVAN. It isn't she, but you who doesn't understand. My wife is not that foolish! Trouble is, she's an artist, it's her nature. She can't help that. Sometimes she gets so carried away it's only natural she should let herself go: right, left, nose, ears . . . (*Slapping back and forth,*

ACT III   IN A MUSIC SHOP

lets himself go into a furious, indistinguishable flurry)
You see what I mean?

SHOPKEEPER. (*Totally befuddled*) No!

IVAN. You deal with artists. You know them. What I'm asking you is a matter of principle. Does she have to use her hands while bawling me out? Just bad manners. That's what it is. And all because she's not exactly what you would call a real blue-blood. In her family closet you can find quite a few skeletons, and in her family album there is an uncle with the face of a real pirate . . . to be sure with no knife in his mouth, but he's got a patched eye. You can't fool me. And let me tell you something more. When I was introduced to her a few years ago I happened to be in a situation where her little inheritance was of primary consideration . . . Not that money means anything to me . . . there was always plenty of that in my life . . . My father, of French and Italian descent was the richest man in town and he left me quite a fortune. But to be honest I was a little too much of a playboy . . . roulette, cards, horses, and especially women . . . hundreds of them . . . running after me . . . pulling at my coattails . . . I had to insult them to get rid of them! (*He throws his leg forward*) Get the hell out of my way! (*Feels pain in his back*)

SHOPKEEPER. (*Worried*) What's the matter? Can I help you?

IVAN. Stay where you belong.

SHOPKEEPER. I'll run to get you a little water.

IVAN. Don't bother. I didn't come to you to be doctored . . . So you see, as I got a little older and after squandering all my money I was ready to fall into my wife's lap . . . She was obviously a woman of considerable appetite which made me think, "What the heck? There'll be plenty of food, a roof over my head and a nice chubby woman in bed . . . Somewhat too chubby for my taste, but with some effort there is no reason why a man even in my condition couldn't make a go of it." And I could . . . But you see, she has a daughter . . . Ah . . . that's a bitter pill. She has a daughter from her first husband. To be precise — from her second husband. She's also an artist. She can't sing, so she plays the piano. She plays . . . (*He laughs*) that is, she tries to play. She tries desperately. All day long . . . with one or two fingers. Bingo-bango, bingo-bango. Then she comes in from the side . . . ahoooo . . . ahoooo. (*He bangs on the counter*) Stop it for heaven's sake! Or that will be the end of all of us—I'm only human.

SHOPKEEPER. (*Bewildered*) I'm sorry . . .

IVAN. You're sorry, but she's stubborn and goes on day in, day out . . . Bingo-bango . . . bingo-bango . . . and from the side . . . ahooo . . . ahooo . . . It was her idea to get the music. It was she who gave me the order, "Take the local train, go to the music shop, ask for the mu-mu . . . ask for the mu-mu . . ." (*He spews out angrily*) You should be ashamed of yourself! . . . What she really needs is not music but a man. She's well on in years and it's about time she stopped banging the piano! But, unfortunately, she's such a homely creature I can't blame the men for staying away from her. Why, I myself, in my early years, couldn't—(*Contemptuously indicating a small woman*) That size . . . and thin as a toothpick . . . and that's not another figure of speech. When I say a toothpick, I actually mean a toothpick . . . (*Indicating*) Nothing here, nothing there. Absolutely a toothpick! Now, how such a mother can have such a daughter is beyond my comprehension. But there they are . . . Now, just imagine my homecoming without the music. My wife grabs me at the door, "Where's the music?" and the toothpick goes right into my eye, "The music!" Now, you go and tell them what happened to the music . . .

ACT III   **IN A MUSIC SHOP**   55

SHOPKEEPER. I admit it's not an enviable situation and believe me, I'm awfully sorry.

IVAN. Why do you keep on telling me you're sorry? I'm surprised at you. It seems you're expecting me to help you instead of you helping me. After all, I'm an old man. I'm not supposed to know much about music. But how is it possible that a man like you should not be able to catch onto a little melody when almost every child on the street knows it . . . sings it . . . dances it.

SHOPKEEPER. If you'd only calm yourself, sir, and try . . .

IVAN. (*In great pain*) I tried. I did try. I told you it starts, "Ah, ah, ah, ah" and then goes into, "Ah, ah, ah, ah".

SHOPKEEPER. Go on . . . go on.

IVAN. Go on where?

SHOPKEEPER. Singing.

IVAN. Singing what?

SHOPKEEPER. It often happens that while humming the wrong melody you stumble onto the one you want. Just go on singing.

IVAN. I knew a million songs in my early days. Surrounded by a flock of good-looking women, I'd stand up in the middle of the room and sing myself hoarse . . . Suppose I try one or two of my old songs on you. I'll start with this one . . . No, I'd better try the other one . . . May I ask you for a glass of water?

SHOPKEEPER. I'm sorry, we have no running water.

IVAN. You see, since my wife does all the singing, I do the listening. And being out of practice for quite a while, your vocal chords get a bit rusty . . . a little, what they call, lubrication might be of some help right now. Please, a glass of water.

SHOPKEEPER. (*With finality*) No water . . .

IVAN. That's all right. Take it easy my friend. I have one or two songs I can do without water. I'll try this one.

SHOPKEEPER. Excuse me . . . If I may suggest . . . perhaps you could try whistling.

IVAN. Oh, God forbid! Whistling is bad luck. I wouldn't allow it in my shop . . . Once I had a friend. He was broke and I took him in. All that man did was whistle. He would walk up and down all day with his hands in his pockets and whistle. It nearly drove me crazy. I was happy when he finally stole some money from my pocket and disappeared. Oh no! God preserve you from friends who whistle. Ah. Singing, that's something else entirely! That, I'll certainly try . . . well . . . What would you like to hear?

SHOPKEEPER. (*Firmly*) Anything at all!

IVAN. But you'll have to help me a little.

SHOPKEEPER. Gladly. Gladly. Let's try a few rhythms. Tim-pum-pum, tim-pum-pum . . . Tam-pum-pum, tam-pum-pum.

(IVAN *closes his eyes, and, following the rhythm, slides into the aria from Pagliacci which he proceeds to render with emotion*)

SHOPKEEPER. (*Continued*) (*Excitedly*) Well . . . that's the opera . . .

IVAN. Please, don't interrupt me. It's awfully disconcerting. It's not easy, you know.

SHOPKEEPER. I was just trying to help you. It's from the opera . . .

IVAN. I know what it is. But you keep dragging me down. I have to go up and you're pulling me down. Up and down . . . It's not easy you know.

SHOPKEEPER. I was trying to keep the rhythm.

IVAN. All right. Keep it! But let's do it together.

SHOPKEEPER. Go ahead. Um-pam-pam, um-pam-pam . . .

ACT III IN A MUSIC SHOP 57

IVAN. Um-pam-pam . . . Um-pam-pam . . . (*Suddenly stops with tears in his eyes*) Look. Why are you tormenting me? I told you distinctly I'm not a singer any more. I don't want an opera, I don't like opera, so why do you insist on nagging me with an opera I don't care for?

SHOPKEEPER. My dear sir, I want to help you . . . so that I can sell you the music.

IVAN. Well, that's all I want! Sell me the music, I pay you, I go home and forget you. But why all this nonsense?

SHOPKEEPER. It makes no difference to me what you choose to sing.

IVAN. So sit down and let me do the singing. I can always try something else . . . Sit down! (*Pokes him*) I'll sing for you the one . . . No, I'd better try the other one . . . Look, I asked you for a glass of water.

SHOPKEEPER. I told you, I have no water . . . This is not a restaurant, it's a music store. Perhaps it would be easier to find it with the help of an instrument. Do you play any kind of an instrument? (*Pointing to the instruments in the window*)

IVAN. Of course I do . . . Why didn't you suggest it before? Why did you let me wear myself out? Where is the piano?

SHOPKEEPER. I haven't got a piano yet. I'll have to work the business up a bit to afford a piano. What I meant was that fingers sometimes retain a melody more easily than the memory. And if you . . .

IVAN. But you have no piano . . .

SHOPKEEPER. (*Walks from behind the counter toward the window hung with instruments*) There're plenty of other instruments . . . trumpet, clarinet, guitar, balalaika, and here is a very nice violin!

(*Gives* IVAN *the violin*)

IVAN. Ahhhh . . . Good . . . Of course, I haven't played the violin for a long time . . . As a matter of fact, I had no mind for anything but parties, wine, women, cards . . . Nevertheless I'll give it a try . . . (*Plays a few notes*) Ahhhh, that's some fiddle you have. How much does a violin like this cost?

SHOPKEEPER. Two rubles.

IVAN. Two rubles! My father bought me a violin years ago for twenty-five rubles and it wasn't as good as this one. (*Strokes the strings*) Oh, what a rich, velvety tone. Only two rubles you say? (*He indulges in playing*)

SHOPKEEPER. Yes. Two rubles.

IVAN. (*Continues to play randomly . . . mutters to himself*) You see, if I could come home with this violin . . . My wife singing, her daughter at the piano, that would be a real concerto in C minor. Say! Where are you? I am playing for you!

SHOPKEEPER. (*Carrying the little bench over to* IVAN) I'm listening! I'm listening! You seem very tired. Perhaps you'd better sit down a little.

(*Touches* IVAN's *arm*)

IVAN. Please, don't push. I hate to be pushed around. (*As if suggesting it to himself*) Yes, it seems there is no other alternative than to sit down and do some more playing. (*Sits down, plays a few chords*) If you don't mind, maybe there is something you could put under me to raise me up a little.

SHOPKEEPER. Certainly. By all means. (*Rushes behind the counter, retrieves a stack of music sheets*)

IVAN. My wife's daughter cannot bang out one note on the piano without a few pillows under her seat.

SHOPKEEPER. Will this be enough?

IVAN. Oh yes . . .

(SHOPKEEPER *puts music on the bench*)

IVAN. (*Continued*) Makes all the difference in the world . . . Now I can really play . . . (*He tries again, turns to see what effect he has made on the* SHOPKEEPER. *Finally he gets up*) Well, nothing, eh?

SHOPKEEPER. (*Gloomily shakes his head*) I'm afraid not.

IVAN. I see the fiddle is not much help to you either . . . Well then, there is no use trying. I'll just have to go home without the music. (*Returns violin. Goes to table to pick up packages*)

SHOPKEEPER. (*Sadly*) I hate to lose a customer.

IVAN. You can't say I haven't tried. I sang. I played. What more do you want of me? There is nothing more I can do but say good-bye and ask your forgiveness for taking up so much of your time.

SHOPKEEPER. I'd do anything to help you . . . It's a shame to let you go like this.

IVAN. I know. You're a kindhearted man and I took advantage of your kindness because, believe me, I'm desperate.

SHOPKEEPER. No use upsetting yourself. It could happen to anyone.

IVAN. I know. But that's no excuse in my house. What could happen to anybody, must not happen to me . . . You see, I was hanging by a thread last week. She gave me only one more chance. And now, if I come home without the music . . . that's the end of the world. "You fool! You imbecile! What are you good for? You are good for nothing! Nowhere! Never! Neither by day nor by night!" . . . And the way she says it would make an ordinary sailor blush. "Get out of my house! Out of my bed! No food, no drink today!" And believe it or not I really get no food. I lay myself down, hungry, in a corner and through the wall I can hear her daughter crying pitifully. And my heart goes out to her. A homely creature . . . lonely . . . Perhaps even lonelier than I am.

At least if she were able to play the piano . . . But not even that! . . . She sits by herself in a darkened room with tears rolling down her cheeks and tries to play with one or two fingers. (*He imitates her, accompanying himself on the counter top*) Ti — ra — ti — ra —

(*The* SHOPKEEPER *joins in*)

SHOPKEEPER. Ti — rata — Ti — rata — Ti —
IVAN. That's the music!
SHOPKEEPER. Is that the music she wants?
IVAN. Quick! Get the music before we forget it. Ti — ra — ti — ra —
SHOPKEEPER. That's the "Waltz of the Manchurian Steppes". Ti — rata — Ti — rata —
IVAN. I don't care what waltz it is. You get the music. I'll do the playing.
SHOPKEEPER. (*Gets the music*) Here it is! Ti — rata — Ti — rata — Ti
IVAN. How much does it cost? Ti — ra — Ti — ra —
SHOPKEEPER. Eighty kopeks. Ti — rata — ta — rata —
IVAN. (*Pays him*) You certainly saved my life! And I can never repay you for that. Here. Take it. (*Hands him a silver coin*) And keep the change.
SHOPKEEPER. Thank you.
IVAN. Thank you.
SHOPKEEPER. And please . . . come again.
IVAN. Absolutely.

THE END

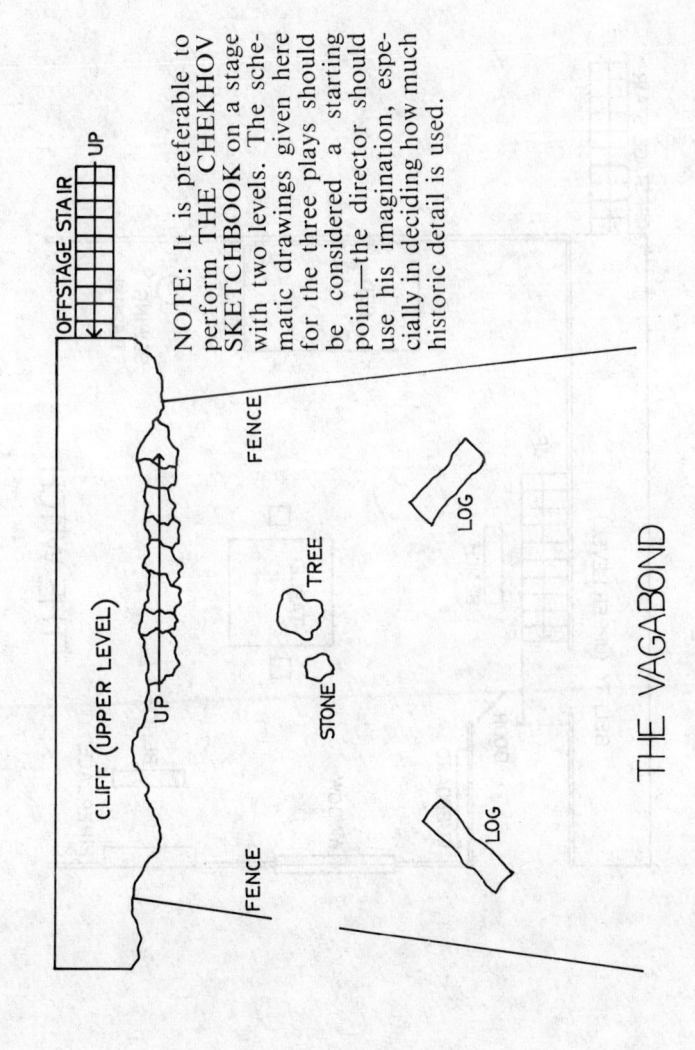

NOTE: It is preferable to perform THE CHEKHOV SKETCHBOOK on a stage with two levels. The schematic drawings given here for the three plays should be considered a starting point—the director should use his imagination, especially in deciding how much historic detail is used.

THE VAGABOND

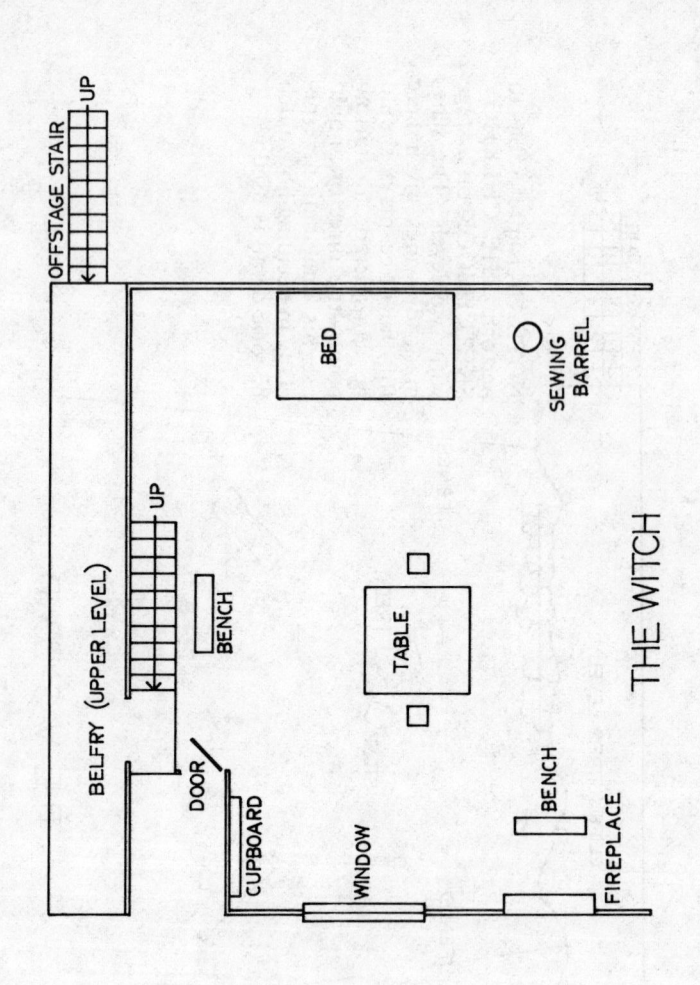

THE WITCH

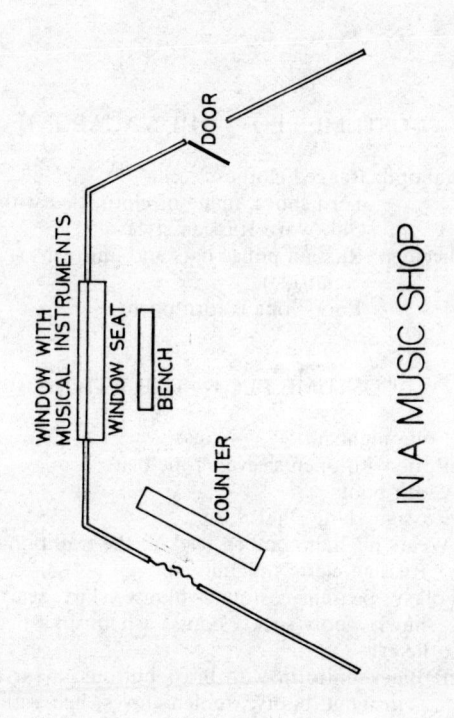

IN A MUSIC SHOP

- WINDOW WITH MUSICAL INSTRUMENTS
- WINDOW SEAT
- BENCH
- COUNTER
- DOOR

COSTUME PLOT—THE VAGABOND

The Vagabond: Ragged clothes
Torn shoes, made of cloth, tied with rope
Old, worn Russian-style cap
The Policemen: Russian police hats and uniforms (fur on the outside)
Boots: one is torn open

COSTUME PLOT—THE WITCH

Savely: Long nightshirt
Robe with open sleeves, rope belt
Cloth boots
Russian cleric's hat
Wears his hair combed back in the traditional Russian cleric's pigtail
Raisa: Folksy, peasant costume—blouse, skirt, scarf, apron, shawl, wooly socks, boots; a babushka tied behind the ears
Postman: Black uniform with brass buttons; a fur cap with insignia; boots; woolen gloves; belt with a heavy buckle; he is covered with snow

COSTUME PLOT—IN A MUSIC SHOP

Shopkeeper: Black boots, pants and vest
Russian peasant shirt—standing collar, buttons on the side, flowers on the front panel
Ivan: Elegantly dressed in a white suit, straw hat, a small necktie, black shoes

PROPERTY LIST—THE VAGABOND

For the Vagabond:
   Chains running from his waist to his legs

For the 2 Policemen:
   2 swords
   2 police whistles on red rope around their necks
   2 revolvers
   Transport orders (carried in Nik's cap)
   Pouch of tobacco and matches
   A few pre-rolled cigarettes may be concealed in the tobacco pouch or in their pockets

PROPERTY LIST—THE WITCH

Kerosene lamp (on table) with an improvised paper shade
Plates, earthenware cups, teakettle, glasses (on shelf)
Broom
Kindling wood
Poker for fire
Small wooden table
Several small benches and tabourets around the table (and where needed)
Large, double couch-bed
Triptych, icons, votive candles (on shelf)
Stove—the fire can light the faces
Old patchwork blankets, cushions
Sewing for Raisa—patchwork quilts, plaids, big needles with heavy thread
Breakable plates, pots, kettles, etc., for Raisa's rage
Two large sacks of mail, covered with snow (carried on by mailman) (Continued on page 66)

PROPERTY LIST—THE WITCH (Continued)

Snow (for entrances and exits in the storm) to put on clothes
Black bread and tea
Several pegs in the wall for hanging coats
A barrel for Raisa's sewing paraphernalia and material
Large keys (to the church) hang on a peg on the wall
A fan may be used for a wind effect when the door is open
A heavy door and a door-bar should be heard Offstage, as indicated

SOUND NOTES:

Chimes on the horse's neck can be heard Offstage, as indicated

Howling winds should be heard throughout

The church bells are represented by 2 ropes in the belfry—the bells are not visible; the sound should be like chimes being struck

PROPERTY LIST—IN A MUSIC SHOP

Flower pot with flowers—on a stand near the door
Old instruments on display in window: violin, trumpet, clarinet, guitar, balalaika
Shelves with sheets of music—some usable, some with Russian titles; in addition, 2 packs of old, used sheets of music for Ivan to sit on
Cat—in a basket on the counter
Bell—hangs over the door, rings when door is opened and closed
Packages—about ten little ones, wrapped and tied (Ivan carries them on)
Change purse with coins—Ivan's personal prop

Other Publications for Your Interest

PASTORAL
(COMEDY)
By PETER MALONEY

1 man, 1 woman—Exterior

Daniel Stern ("Blue Thunder", "Breaking Away") and Kristin Griffith ("The Europeans", "Interiors") starred originally at NYC's famed Ensemble Studio Theatre in the preceptive comedy about a city couple temporarily tending a farm. He hates the bucolic life and is terrified, for instance, by such horrors as a crowing rooster; whereas she is at one with the land *and* the rooster. "An endearing picture of young love at a comic crossroads."—N.Y. Times. "Sharp, satiric humor."—New Yorker. "An audience pleaser."—Village Voice. Published with *Last Chance Texaco*. (#17995)

(Royalty, $15–$10.)

LAST CHANCE TEXACO
(DRAMA)
By PETER MALONEY

3 women—Interior

Originally staged to great acclaim at NYC's famed Ensemble Studio Theatre, this is a haunting, lyrical play set in the American Garage, a Texaco station in a small Texas town run by a mother and her daughter. Late one night, while driving through, a city woman named Ruth has a flat tire, an occurrence which causes her own unusual life to intersect with Verna and Cissy, as they fix her tire in the American Garage. This play is an excellent source of monologue and scene material. It is also a gripping piece of theatre. Published with *Pastoral*. (#13887)

(Royalty, $15–$10.)

BUSINESSMAN'S LUNCH
(COMEDY)
By MICHAEL QUINN

4 men, 1 woman—Interior

Originally produced by the famed Actors Theatre of Louisville, this marked the debut of a wonderful new comic playwriting voice. We are in one of those quiche-and-salad restaurants, where three high-powered young executives of a nearby candy company are having lunch as they discuss company politics and various marketing and advertising strategies. They particularly enjoy making fun of one of their fellows who is not present, whom they consider a hopeless nerd—until, that is, they learn that he is engaged to marry the boss's daughter. "Cleverly skewers corporate stereotypes."—NY Times. (#4712)

(Royalty, $20–$15.)

#W-36

Other Publications for Your Interest

THE SQUARE ROOT OF LOVE
(ALL GROUPS—FOUR COMEDIES)
By DANIEL MELTZER

1 man, 1 woman—4 Simple Interiors

This full-length evening portrays four preludes to love—from youth to old age, from innocence to maturity. Best when played by a single actor and actress. **The Square Root of Love.** Two genius-level college students discover that Man (or Woman) does not live by intellectual pursuits alone . . . **A Good Time for a Change.** Our couple are now a successful executive and her handsome young male secretary. He has decided it's time for a change, and so has she . . . **The Battling Brinkmires.** George and Marsha Brinkmire, a middle-aged couple, have come to Haiti to get a "quickie" divorce. This one has a surprise ending . . . **Waiting For To Go.** We are on a jet waiting to take off for Florida. He's a retired plumbing contractor who thinks his life is over—she's a recent widow returning to her home in Hallandale. The play, and the evening, ends with a beginning . . . A success at off-off Broadway's Hunter Playwrights. Requires only minimal settings.   (#21314)

(Royalty, $50-$35. Each play separately: $15-$10.)

SNOW LEOPARDS
(LITTLE THEATRE—COMIC DRAMA)
By MARTIN JONES

2 women—Exterior

This haunting little gem of a play was a recent crowd-pleaser Off Off Broadway in New York City, produced by the fine StageArts Theatre Co. Set in Lincoln Park Zoo in Chicago in front of the snow leopards' pen, the play tells the story of two sisters from rural West Virginia. When we first meet Sally, she has run away from home to find her big sister Claire June, whose life Up North she has imagined to be filled with all the promise and hopes so lacking Down Home. Turns out, life in the Big City ain't all Sally and C.J. thought it would be: but Sally is going to stay anyway, and try to make her way. "Affecting and carefully crafted . . . a moving piece of work."—New York City Tribune. *Actresses take note*: this play is a treasure trove of scene and monologue material. *Producers take note*: the play may be staged simply and inexpensively.   (#21245)

(Royalty, $50-$35. *Note*: the first act may be produced *solus*,
also under the title *Snow Leopards*, for a royalty of $25-$20.)